Collins

easy learning

Telling the time

Ages 5–7

Ian Jacques

How to use this book

- Find a quiet, comfortable place to work, away from distractions.
- Tackle one topic at a time.
- Help with reading the instructions where necessary and ensure that your child understands what to do.
- Discuss with your child what they have learnt.
- Let your child return to their favourite pages once they have been completed, to talk about the activities.
- Reward your child with plenty of praise and encouragement.

Although digital times may not have been covered in the classroom, the concept of digital times are introduced in this book to aid recognition and familiarity. Help your child with these questions where needed. All digital times are treated as morning (AM) times.

Special features

- Yellow boxes: Introduce and outline the key ideas in each section.
- Orange shaded boxes: Offer advice to parents on how to consolidate your child's understanding.
- Game: There is a game provided at the end of the book to reinforce the whole topic.

Published by Collins
An imprint of HarperCollins*Publishers*
1 London Bridge Street
London SE1 9GF

Browse the complete Collins catalogue at www.collins.co.uk

© HarperCollins*Publishers* 2011
This edition © HarperCollins*Publishers* 2015

20

ISBN 978-0-00-813437-2

The publisher wishes to thank the following for permission to use copyright material: p4 © Matthew Cole/shutterstock.com, © Kimazo/shutterstock.com

The author asserts their moral rights to be identified as the author of this work.

British Library Cataloguing in Publication Data

A Catalogue record for this publication is available from the British Library

Written by Ian Jacques
Contributors: Adam Blackwood and Melissa Blackwood
Composition by Linda Miles, Lodestone Publishing Ltd and Contentra Technologies
Illustrated by Graham Smith
Cover design by Sarah Duxbury and Paul Oates
Cover illustration by Kathy Baxendale
Project managed by Chantal Peacock and Sonia Dawkins
Printed in Great Britain by Bell and Bain Ltd, Glasgow

Contents

Times of day

1 Draw a line to join the start of the sentence to the picture that completes it.

The first thing I do in the morning is........

Next I have to.......

After breakfast I.......

Before the afternoon comes I eat my........

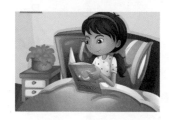

In the evening I read a........

Finally it is time to........

For most children, morning is the period between getting up and lunchtime, afternoon is the period between lunch and dinner / tea time and evening takes them through until bedtime.

2 Write the words **morning**, **afternoon** or **evening** in the spaces.

I go to bed in the _____.

I eat my breakfast in the _____.

I come home from school in the _____.

I brush my teeth in the _____ and _____.

The sun sets in the _____.

My last birthday party took place in the _____.

3 Draw a picture to show something that you did **yesterday**, something you did **today** and something you would like to do **tomorrow**.

Yesterday	Today	Tomorrow

When talking to your child about future plans or recalling what has come before use the language of 'tomorrow', 'yesterday', 'the day after tomorrow', 'one week ago', 'a fortnight's time', etc. to increase their familiarity with such vocabulary.

Days of the week

There are 7 days in a week.

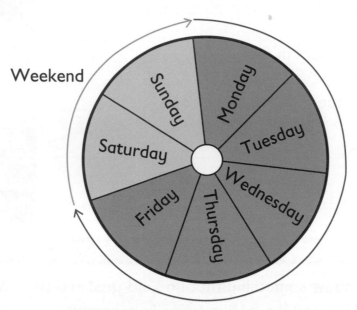

Weekend

1 Fill in the missing days of the week.

If today is Tuesday then tomorrow will be _____.

If today is Sunday then yesterday was _____.

If yesterday was Friday then today is _____.

If tomorrow is Wednesday then today is _____.

The two days of the weekend are _____

and _____.

Monday
Tuesday
Wednesday
Thursday
Friday
Saturday
Sunday

Help your child to become familiar with the days of the week, the order they come in and how to spell them accurately when writing them.

2 Write down the name of your favourite TV programme and a fun activity that you will do each day next week.

Day	TV Programme	Activity
Monday		
Tuesday		
Wednesday		
Thursday		
Friday		
Saturday		
Sunday		

3 Use the table below to help you learn how to spell the days of the week correctly. Start by looking at the word and then read the word aloud. Now read the word one letter at a time and copy down the word. Cover up the word and try to write it down from memory. Finally check your spelling and give yourself a tick if it is correct.

Look and Read	Look and Write	Cover and Write	Check
Monday			
Tuesday			
Wednesday			
Thursday			
Friday			
Saturday			
Sunday			

Months and seasons

There are 12 months in a year.
The year begins with January.

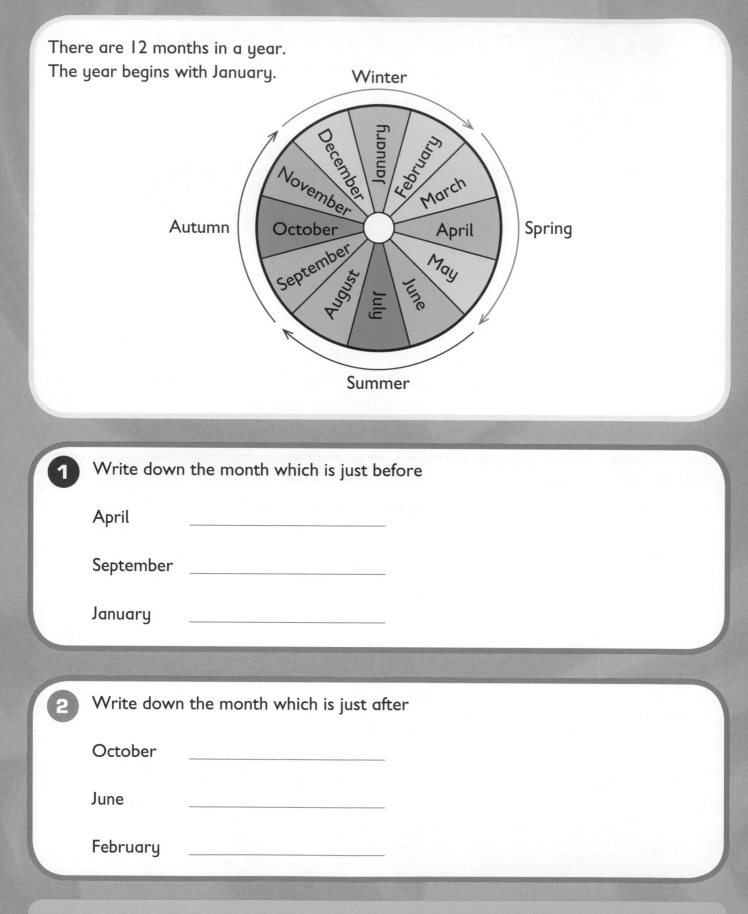

Winter

Autumn

Spring

Summer

1 Write down the month which is just before

April   _____

September   _____

January   _____

2 Write down the month which is just after

October   _____

June   _____

February   _____

Help your child to become familiar with the months of the year, the order they come in and how to spell them accurately when writing them.

3 Write the season under each picture.

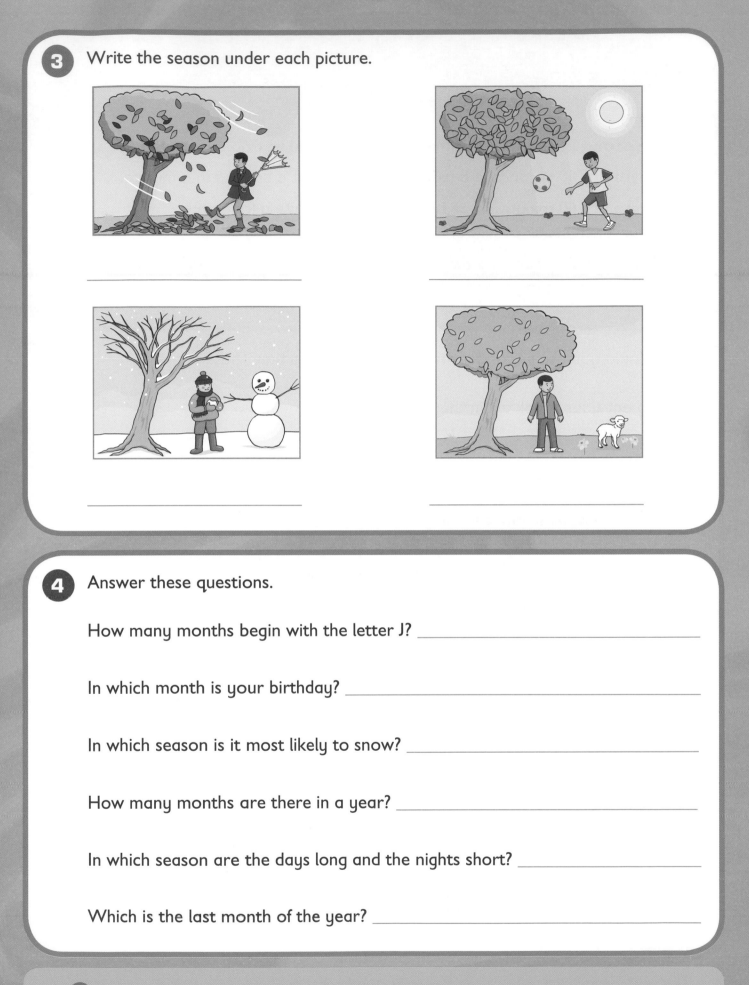

_____   _____

_____   _____

4 Answer these questions.

How many months begin with the letter J? _____

In which month is your birthday? _____

In which season is it most likely to snow? _____

How many months are there in a year? _____

In which season are the days long and the nights short? _____

Which is the last month of the year? _____

Use **3**, as a discussion point with your child; discuss which months fall within these seasons, the key events that occur for your family at these points in the year and which elements of these seasons they particularly enjoy, etc.

Time words

A **second** is a very short time. It takes a second to clap your hands.

There are 60 seconds in a **minute**. You can eat a banana in a minute.

There are 60 minutes in an **hour**. An hour is quite a long time.
Your lunch break at school is about an hour.

There are 24 hours in a **day**. You probably spend around half of those hours awake and the other half asleep.

1 Would you use **seconds**, **minutes** or **hours** to time these activities?

To eat your breakfast in the morning _____

To sneeze _____

Time spent at school each day _____

Use these words to complete the sentences below.

quicker   **slower**   **earlier**   **later**

Tired legs make you run _____ than usual.

Babies' bedtimes are _____ than adults' bedtimes.

A minute passes _____ than an hour.

If you wanted to sleep in, you would set your alarm for _____ than usual.

Try asking your child to close their eyes and open them again after one minute. Time them to see how good they are at estimating a minute. You can make this into a fun game.

2 How many times can you do each of these activities in 1 **minute**?

Jump up and down on the spot _____

Write your name _____

Put one sock on and off again _____

Count up to ten _____

3 Write the following lengths of time in the boxes below, so they go from the **shortest** time to the **longest** time.

12 hours   60 minutes   1 second   1 day   1 week   half an hour

LONGEST
length
of time

SHORTEST
length
of time

Support your child in completing **2** by acting as time keeper as they complete each task. Then swap roles and see who does best.

On the hour times

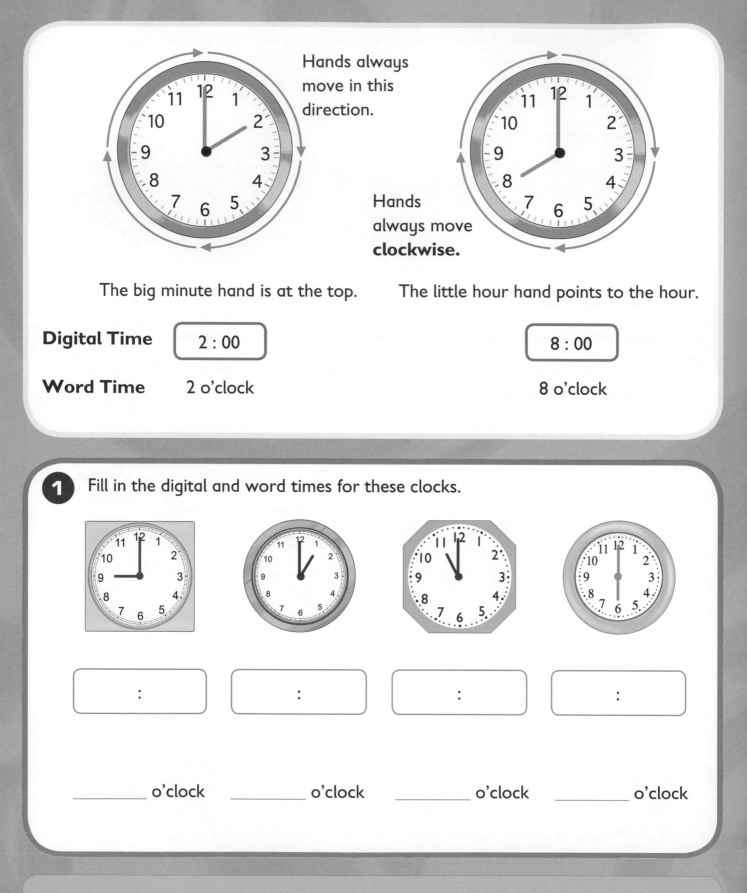

Hands always move in this direction.

The big minute hand is at the top.

Hands always move **clockwise.**

The little hour hand points to the hour.

Digital Time   2 : 00

8 : 00

Word Time   2 o'clock

8 o'clock

1 Fill in the digital and word times for these clocks.

:   :   :   :

_____ o'clock   _____ o'clock   _____ o'clock   _____ o'clock

Use a real clock or watch at home and make the times relevant to your child by showing them the time on the clock when they go to bed, leave the house to go to school and so on.

2 Fill in the missing word times.

4 : 00		12 : 00

_____ o'clock   _____ o'clock

5 : 00		6 : 00

_____ o'clock   _____ o'clock

3 Fill in the missing digital times.

:	:	:	:

2 o'clock   10 o'clock   7 o'clock   3 o'clock

4 Put these in time order and then use the letters under each clock to spell a mystery word. Start with 3 o'clock.

G   A   I   M   C

The word is _____ _____ _____ _____ _____.

13

Half past times

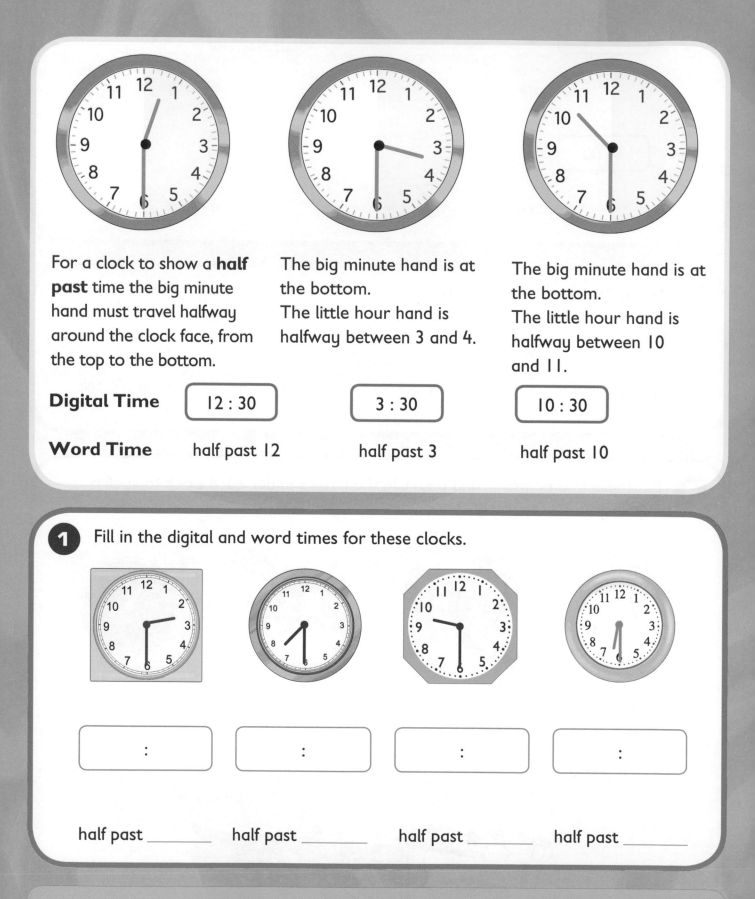

For a clock to show a **half past** time the big minute hand must travel halfway around the clock face, from the top to the bottom.

The big minute hand is at the bottom.
The little hour hand is halfway between 3 and 4.

The big minute hand is at the bottom.
The little hour hand is halfway between 10 and 11.

Digital Time

12 : 30

3 : 30

10 : 30

Word Time

half past 12

half past 3

half past 10

1 Fill in the digital and word times for these clocks.

:

:

:

:

half past _____   half past _____   half past _____   half past _____

Use a real clock and move the hand round from 4 o'clock to half past 4 and then on to 5 o'clock. Point out what happens to both hands when you do this. Show your child that as the big hand passes the bottom the little hand is halfway between the 4 and 5. Repeat this for other times.

2 Fill in the missing word times.

| 12 : 30 |

half past _____

| 1 : 30 |

half past _____

| 4 : 30 |

half past _____

| 8 : 30 |

half past _____

3 Fill in the missing digital times.

| : | | : | | : | | : |

half past 9   half past 3   half past 11   half past 5

4 What time will it be one hour later than the time shown.

| 9 : 30 | ? | : |

| 6 : 30 | ? | : |

| 2 : 30 | ? | : |

| 7 : 30 | ? | : |

| 10 : 30 | ? | : |

If your child is not confident with the concept of 'a half', get them to stand up and make a 'half turn' or cut a circle of paper into two halves.

Practice questions

Write down the missing digital and word times for these clocks.

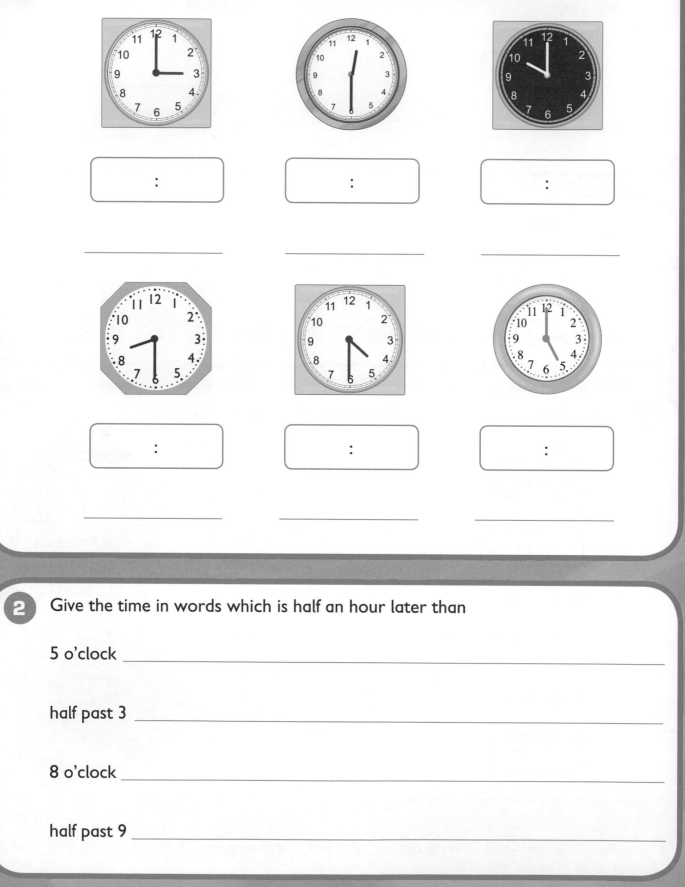

```
 :          :          :
```

```
 :          :          :
```

2 Give the time in words which is half an hour later than

5 o'clock _____

half past 3 _____

8 o'clock _____

half past 9 _____

3 Each row shows the time every half hour. Fill in the missing times.

| 2 : 00 | 2 : 30 | 3 : 00 | : |

| 5 : 30 | 6 : 00 | 6 : 30 | : |

| 3 : 00 | 3 : 30 | : | 4 : 30 |

| 10 : 00 | : | 11 : 00 | 11 : 30 |

| : | 9 : 00 | 9 : 30 | : |

4 How many hours are there between

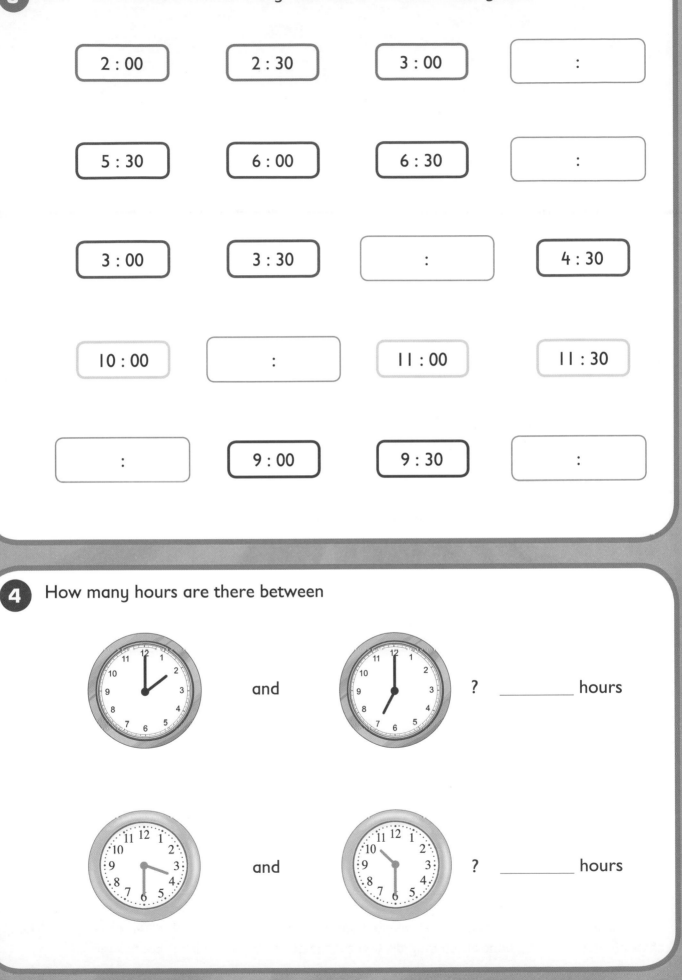

and   ? _____ hours

and   ? _____ hours

17

Putting hands on the clock

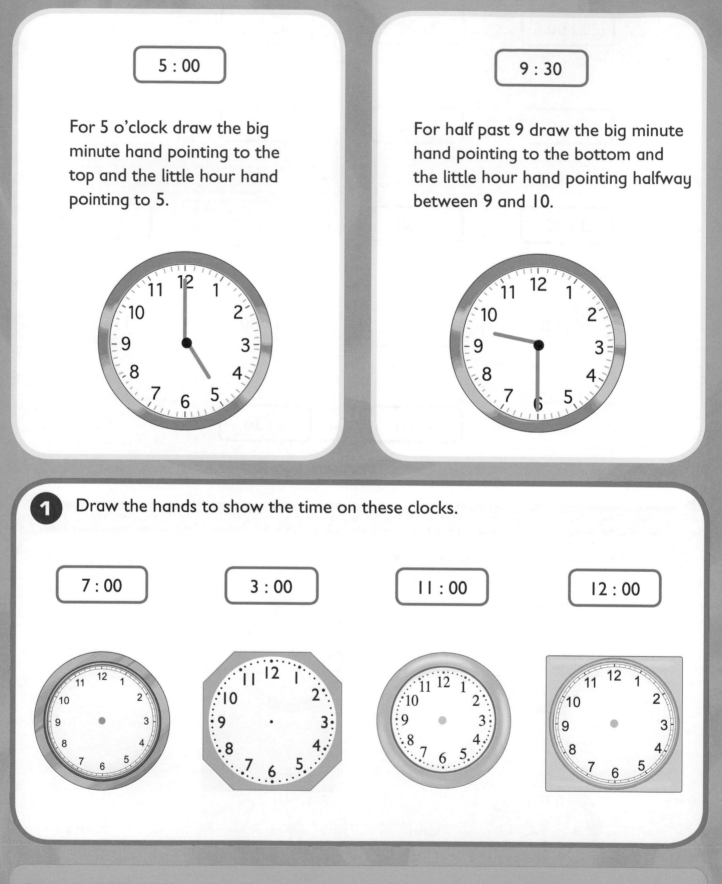

5 : 00

For 5 o'clock draw the big minute hand pointing to the top and the little hour hand pointing to 5.

9 : 30

For half past 9 draw the big minute hand pointing to the bottom and the little hour hand pointing halfway between 9 and 10.

1 Draw the hands to show the time on these clocks.

7 : 00

3 : 00

11 : 00

12 : 00

Encourage your child to draw the big minute hand and little hour hand with different lengths. When children first draw the hands they may draw them the same length, which is confusing.

18

2 Draw the hands to show the time on these clocks.

1 : 30 4 : 30 12 : 30 10 : 30

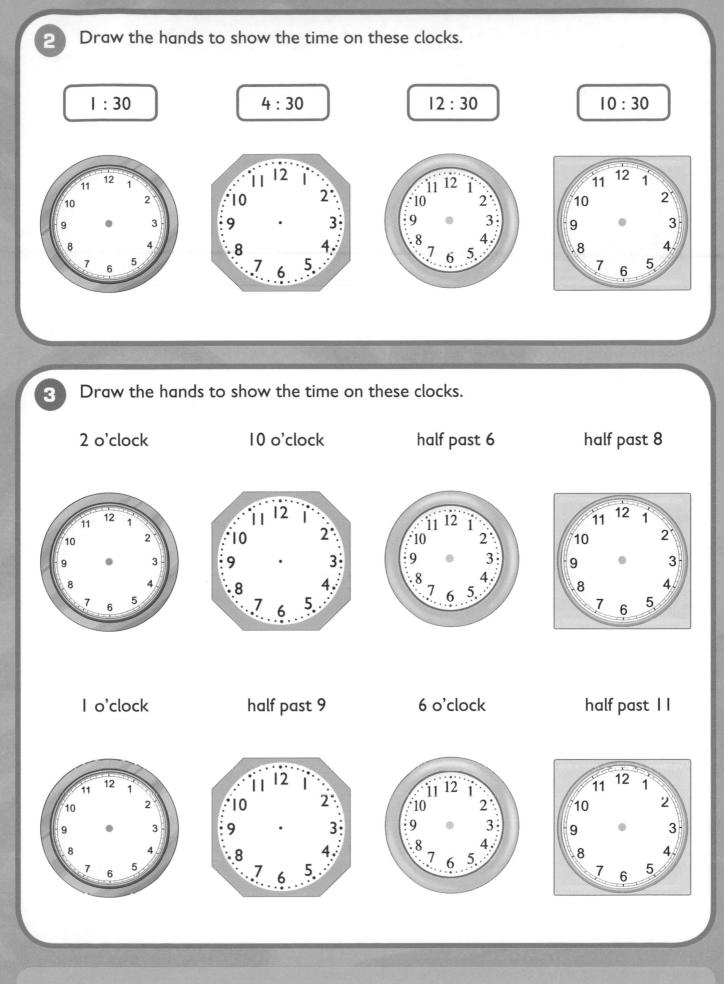

3 Draw the hands to show the time on these clocks.

2 o'clock   10 o'clock   half past 6   half past 8

1 o'clock   half past 9   6 o'clock   half past 11

When drawing the half past times check that the little hand has been drawn in the correct position.

19

Quarter past times

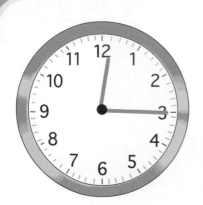 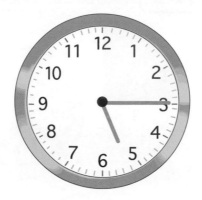 

For a clock to show a **quarter past** time the big minute hand must travel one-quarter of the way around the clock face.

The big minute hand points to the right.
The little hour hand is just past the 5 on its way to the 6.

The big minute hand points to the right.
The little hour hand is just past the 9 on its way to the 10.

Digital Time

12 : 15

5 : 15

9 : 15

Word Time   quarter past 12   quarter past 5   quarter past 9

---

1   Fill in the digital and word times for these clocks.

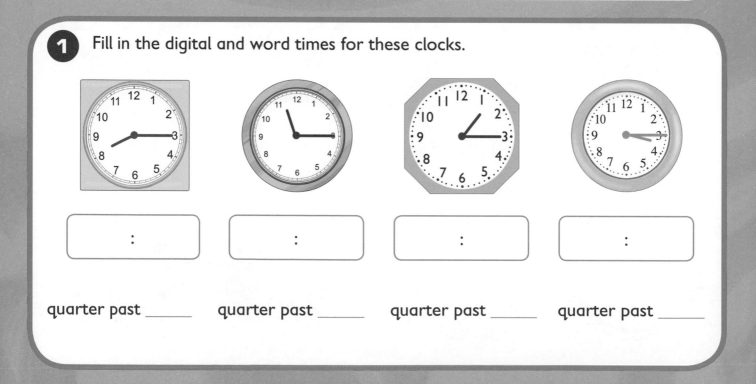

:   :   :   :

quarter past _____   quarter past _____   quarter past _____   quarter past _____

Move the hands of a real clock from 5 o'clock to quarter past 5 and notice that the little hand has moved towards the 6 but only by a small amount.

2 Fill in the missing word times.

4 : 15		1 : 15

quarter past _____   quarter past _____

7 : 15		10 : 15

quarter past _____   quarter past _____

3 Fill in the missing digital times.

:	:	:	:

quarter past 12   quarter past 2   quarter past 6   quarter past 1

4 The rabbit wants to hop home to its burrow through the cabbage patch.
Find a path by colouring in all of the cabbages which show quarter past times.

11:15   1:15   8:15   11:15

12:15

4:15   3:00   6:30

2:15

9:15   4:00   2:30

12:30

5:15

Quarter to times

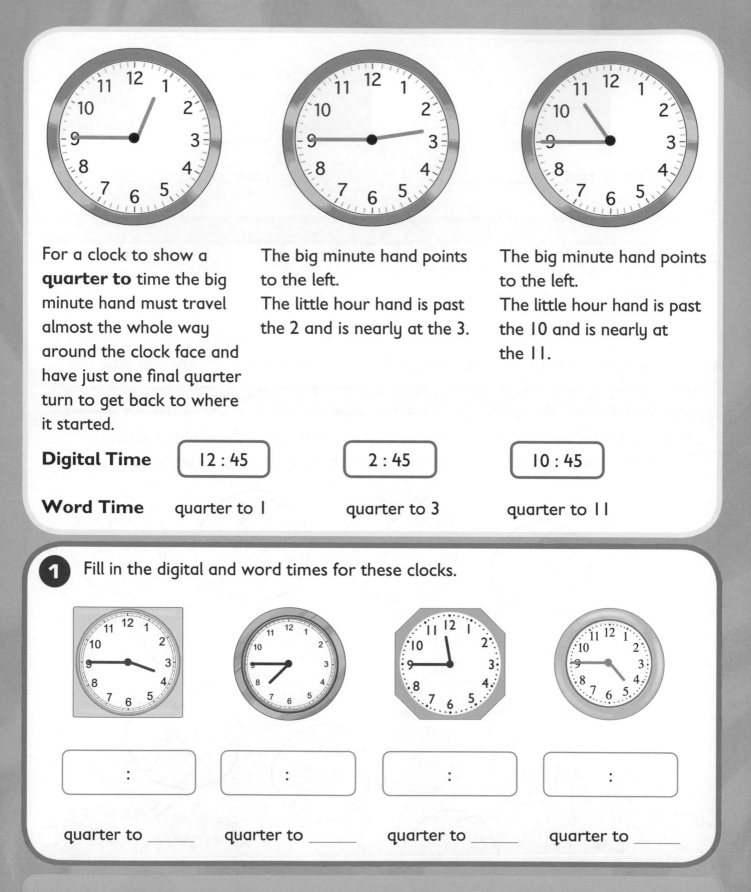

For a clock to show a **quarter to** time the big minute hand must travel almost the whole way around the clock face and have just one final quarter turn to get back to where it started.

The big minute hand points to the left.
The little hour hand is past the 2 and is nearly at the 3.

The big minute hand points to the left.
The little hour hand is past the 10 and is nearly at the 11.

Digital Time

| 12 : 45 | 2 : 45 | 10 : 45 |

Word Time

quarter to 1   quarter to 3   quarter to 11

---

1   Fill in the digital and word times for these clocks.

| : | : | : | : |

quarter to _____   quarter to _____   quarter to _____   quarter to _____

Children find it hard to understand why 2:45 is quarter to 3 and not quarter to 2. Move the hands round a real clock from 2:30 to 2:45 to 3:00 and point out that at 2:45 there is just one quarter turn to go to get to 3:00.

2 Fill in the missing word times.

8 : 45

quarter to _____

1 : 45

quarter to _____

5 : 45

quarter to _____

11 : 45

quarter to _____

3 Fill in the missing digital times.

| : | : | : | : |

quarter to 7   quarter to 3   quarter to 9   quarter to 1

4 Fill in the missing numbers in this time machine. The first one has been done for you.

4 : 15

7 : 45

2 : 45

5 : 15

9 : 45

half an hour later

4 : 45

:

:

:

:

Other past times

The clock can be easily split into 5 minute sections. When the big minute hand moves from the 12 around to the 1 it takes 5 minutes, to get to the 2 takes 10 minutes, to get to 3 takes 15 minutes and so on. Between the o'clock and half past we read these 5 minute chunks as 'past' times, so:

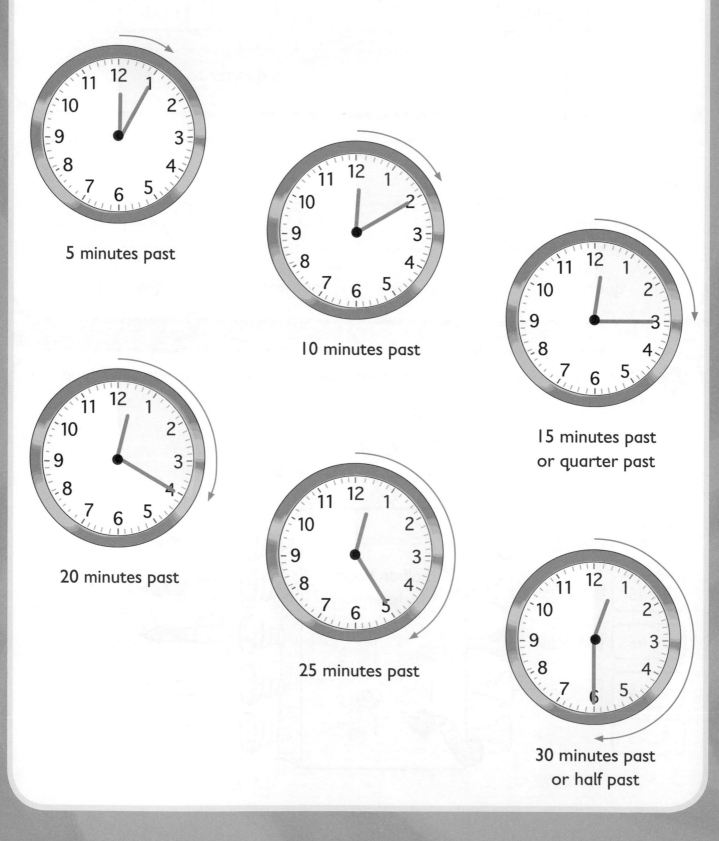

5 minutes past

10 minutes past

15 minutes past
or quarter past

20 minutes past

25 minutes past

30 minutes past
or half past

1 On the clock below, fill in how many 'minutes past' it will be when the big minute hand gets to each point.

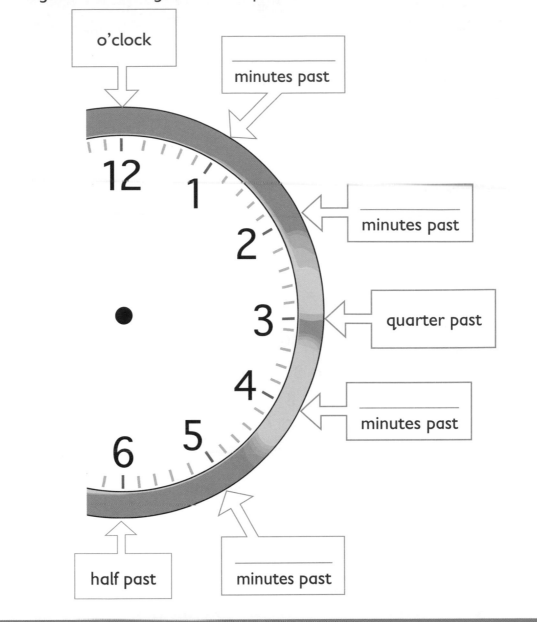

o'clock

_____ minutes past

_____ minutes past

quarter past

_____ minutes past

half past

_____ minutes past

2 Write the times shown under these clocks. The first one has been done for you.

20 minutes
past 11

_____   _____   _____

_____   _____   _____

25

Other to times

As we have seen, the clock can be easily split into 5 minute sections so we can count how many minutes it is until the next o'clock time. We do this between half past and o'clock times, counting the 5 minute sections left until the big minute hand gets back to the top. We read these times as 'to' times.

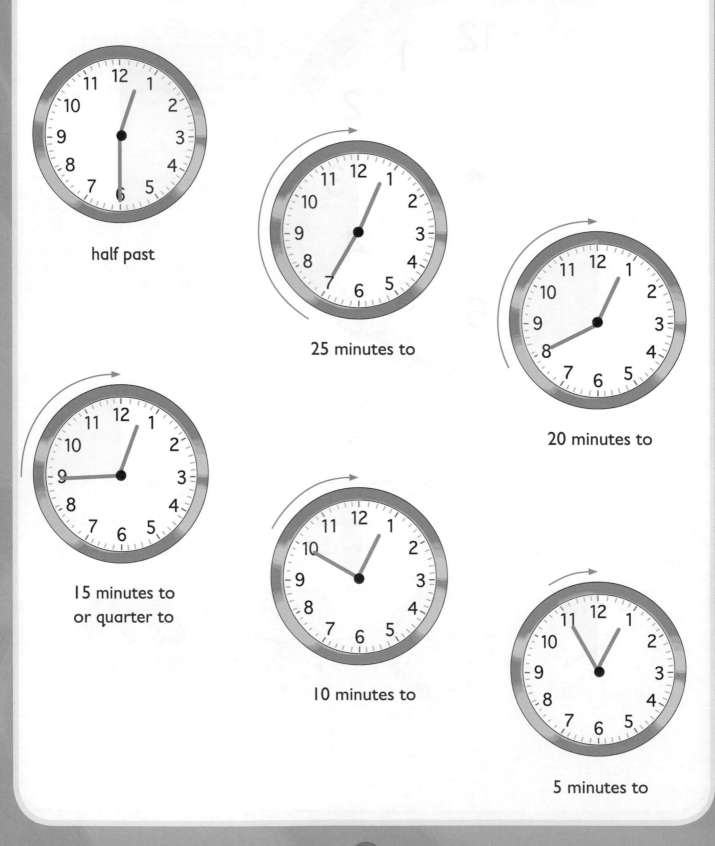

half past

25 minutes to

20 minutes to

15 minutes to
or quarter to

10 minutes to

5 minutes to

1 On the clock below, fill in how many 'minutes to' the next o'clock time it will be when the big minute hand gets to each point.

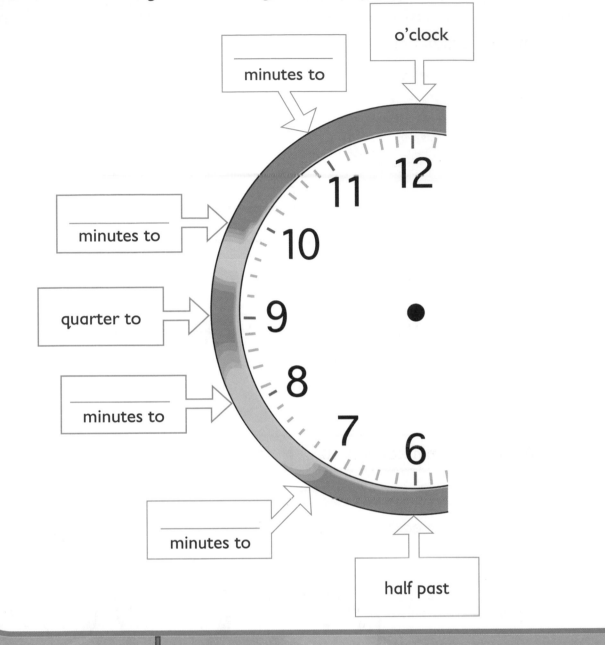

| o'clock |
| _____ minutes to |
| _____ minutes to |
| quarter to |
| _____ minutes to |
| _____ minutes to |
| half past |

2 Write the times shown under these clocks. The first one has been done for you.

10 minutes to 4

_____   _____   _____

Practice questions

1 Fill in the missing digital times.

   :   :   :   :

2 Draw the minute hands on the clocks to show the correct times.

9 : 00   10 minutes past 10   3 : 15   5 minutes to 2

3 Draw a string to match each child with their balloon.

4 : 45   12 : 00   2 : 15   9 : 50   3 : 30

4 Write down these times in words.

| 6 : 30 | 8 : 00 | 11 : 15 |

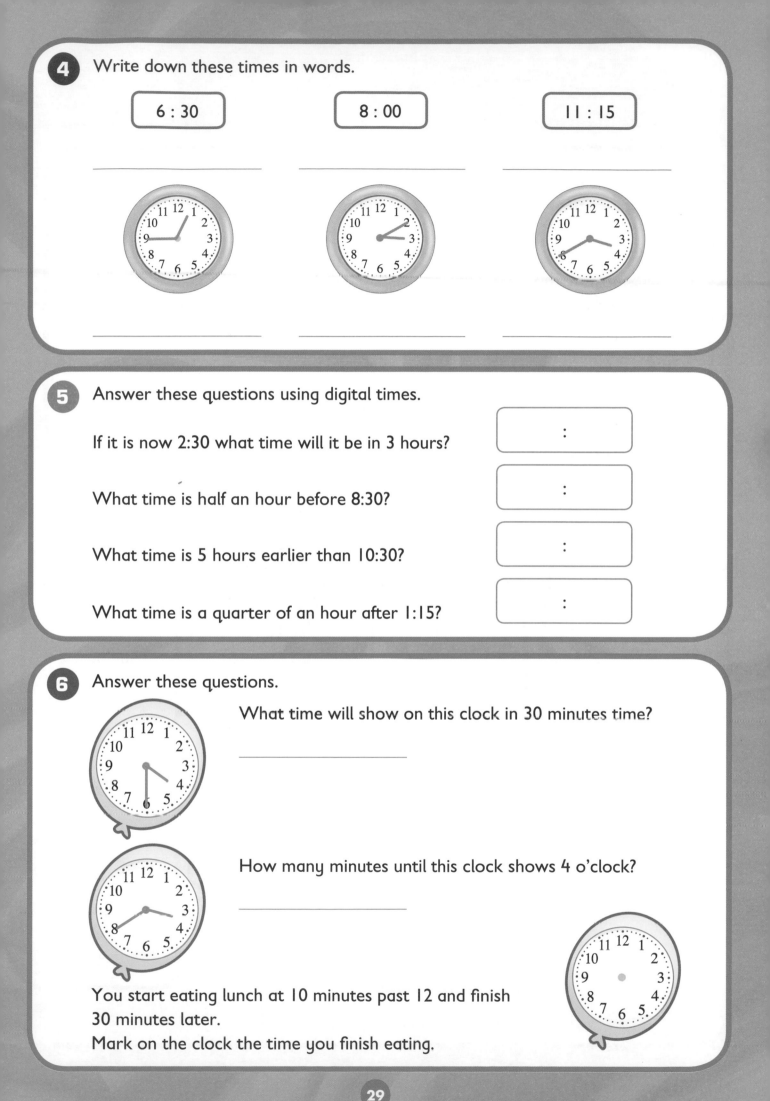

_____   _____   _____

_____   _____   _____

5 Answer these questions using digital times.

If it is now 2:30 what time will it be in 3 hours?

What time is half an hour before 8:30?

What time is 5 hours earlier than 10:30?

What time is a quarter of an hour after 1:15?

6 Answer these questions.

What time will show on this clock in 30 minutes time?

_____

How many minutes until this clock shows 4 o'clock?

_____

You start eating lunch at 10 minutes past 12 and finish
30 minutes later.
Mark on the clock the time you finish eating.

Pairs game

You need: either counters to cover up the squares or copy the cards, cut them out and place them face down on a table or floor.

Rules:

- Take turns at choosing a pair of cards, either by moving the counters off the cards or by turning them over.
- If the cards show matching times, then you win them.
- If they are not matching times, turn them back over (or cover with counters) and the next person picks a pair.
- The person with the most pairs at the end of the game wins.

10 minutes to 5

half past 7

6 : 00

20 minutes past 2

6 o'clock

2 : 30

half past 2

quarter past 5

7 : 30

4 : 15

quarter to 8

8 : 15

quarter to 4

4 : 45

11 : 45

Answers

The answers to all questions involving digital times are given as morning (AM) times but 24 hour clock times are also acceptable.

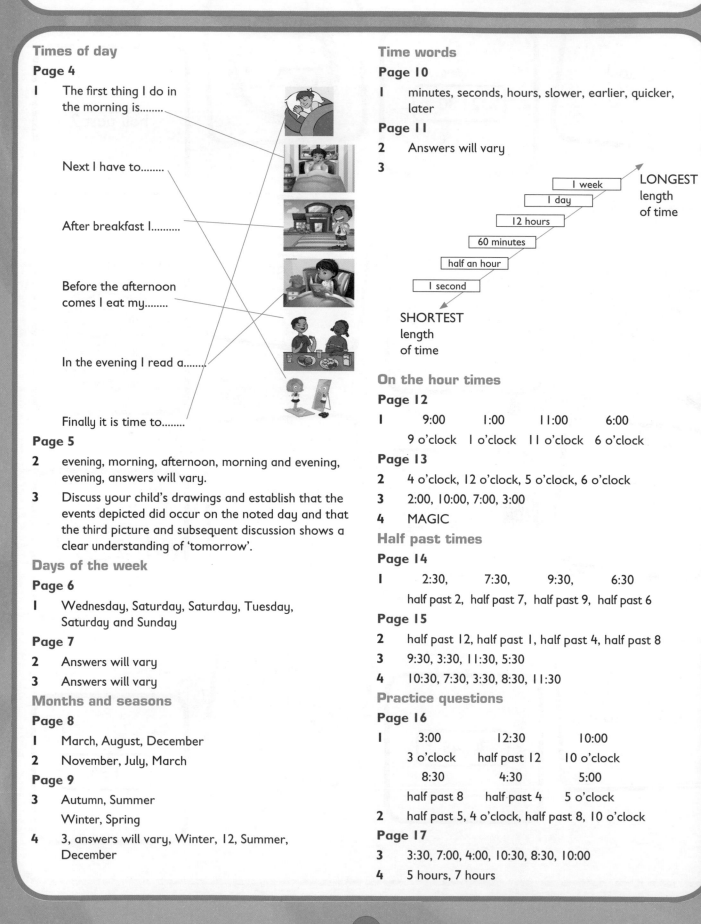

Times of day

Page 4

1 The first thing I do in the morning is........

Next I have to........

After breakfast I..........

Before the afternoon comes I eat my........

In the evening I read a........

Finally it is time to........

Page 5

2 evening, morning, afternoon, morning and evening, evening, answers will vary.

3 Discuss your child's drawings and establish that the events depicted did occur on the noted day and that the third picture and subsequent discussion shows a clear understanding of 'tomorrow'.

Days of the week

Page 6

1 Wednesday, Saturday, Saturday, Tuesday, Saturday and Sunday

Page 7

2 Answers will vary

3 Answers will vary

Months and seasons

Page 8

1 March, August, December

2 November, July, March

Page 9

3 Autumn, Summer
   Winter, Spring

4 3, answers will vary, Winter, 12, Summer, December

Time words

Page 10

1 minutes, seconds, hours, slower, earlier, quicker, later

Page 11

2 Answers will vary

3

LONGEST length of time

1 week

1 day

12 hours

60 minutes

half an hour

1 second

SHORTEST length of time

On the hour times

Page 12

1 9:00   1:00   11:00   6:00
   9 o'clock 1 o'clock 11 o'clock 6 o'clock

Page 13

2 4 o'clock, 12 o'clock, 5 o'clock, 6 o'clock

3 2:00, 10:00, 7:00, 3:00

4 MAGIC

Half past times

Page 14

1 2:30,   7:30,   9:30,   6:30
   half past 2, half past 7, half past 9, half past 6

Page 15

2 half past 12, half past 1, half past 4, half past 8

3 9:30, 3:30, 11:30, 5:30

4 10:30, 7:30, 3:30, 8:30, 11:30

Practice questions

Page 16

1 3:00   12:30   10:00
   3 o'clock   half past 12   10 o'clock
        8:30   4:30   5:00
   half past 8   half past 4   5 o'clock

2 half past 5, 4 o'clock, half past 8, 10 o'clock

Page 17

3 3:30, 7:00, 4:00, 10:30, 8:30, 10:00

4 5 hours, 7 hours